DALVIN COOK

THE INSPIRATIONAL STORY OF HOW DALVIN COOK MADE IT TO THE NFL

By

JACKSON CARTER

Copyright © 2022

Table of Contents

LEGAL NOTES

Dalvin Cook is meant for entertainment and educational use only. All attempts have been made to present factual information in an unbiased context.

A Long Path To Greatness

It hasn't always been easy for Dalvin Cook.

Yes, he is now considered one of the greatest running backs alive in the NFL. And yes, he was drafted easily by the Minnesota Vikings back in 2016, making him a player to watch for anyone paying attention to the most famous football league in the world.

And yes, he has found great success in the game. Throughout his time in the league, he has proven himself as someone who doesn't only have talent, but also intelligence, drive, and a determination to get better and better. He rose through the ranks of the team and repeatedly showed that he has what it takes. And with each battle he's won and each time he's advanced his team, Dalvin's star has risen bit by bit.

It has now reached the point where Dalvin is nearly a household name. Anyone who actually pays attention to the NFL knows him and every opponent within the league fears him. He is powerful, he is dedicated, he is strong and steadfast, accomplished, and always evolving. There is no doubt that Dalvin Cook is easily one of the greatest football players alive right now.

But no, it hasn't been easy for him.

He has suffered his fair share of setbacks, both personal and related to his career. He has made mistakes—quite a few of them—and lost those close to him along the way.

He has been hurt, has doubted himself and his team, and has sabotaged himself at times too.

When you look at the life and career of Dalvin Cook, you see someone who is supremely talented and able to go all the way in the NFL. You see someone who could someday win a Super Bowl ring or be named MVP. You also see someone who hasn't even reached his full potential yet and still has great room to grow.

And when you look at him, you also see someone who is very human—someone who makes mistakes; someone who doubts himself and often lets the worst of him get the best of him. You see someone who isn't a cookie-cutter hero for young football fans across the nation.

But you also see someone who was raised with respect and care for his family and friends. You see someone who was repeatedly told he could do better. You see someone who is never truly satisfied with his output and is constantly making sure that he can do even more, reach higher, push further, and do better.

Dalvin Cook has made it hard to root for him sometimes. He has made himself look like someone who can overindulge in the worst habits of a professional athlete. He seemed to have gotten lost in his ego, temper, and horrible judgment. There have been numerous times when Cook didn't seem like a hero. Far from it—he actually seemed like a villain.

He is a great reminder that we are all human. Even the most successful people among us have flaws and are a constant work in progress. That is no different for Dalvin Cook, who is trying to be a better man, a better citizen, a better partner, and a better football player.

Is he a work in progress? Yes. But does he have the potential to be not only a great athlete but also a great man? He has all the potential in the world.

Who is Dalvin Cook and what drew him to football? More specifically, what drew him to be the sort of athlete he is today? And what is holding him back and slowing him down? How can he banish those demons, improve his life and personality, overcome his shortcomings, and focus on being a true champion?

Dalvin Cook's road to NFL stardom has been long and, at times, bumpy. But it's well worth studying and understanding. He doesn't come without flaws, but he certainly does come with a fascinating story to tell.

Just Like Dad: Growing Up Dalvin

His path to stardom and success in the NFL started in a colorful and warm corner of Florida. Dalvin grew up in Opa-locka, Florida under the bright sun and close to the warm waters of the coast.

Dalvin grew up as one of six other children in his family. This means that he was hardly ever alone and was always out playing with his siblings and being taught things—both good and bad—by his brothers and sisters. DeAndre Burnett is the oldest of the six kids among Dalvin, Daneshia, James, Jameisha, and Jamiya. Demarcus Cook is yet another son of the family.

From the very beginning, family was very important to Dalvin, and that was because of the way his parents raised him. James and Varondria White may have had their differences and might have had separate, unique approaches to raising their children, but they made one thing clear: family was family and nothing was more important than that.

This was an easy thing to accept and embrace because of the love and close relationship Dalvin had with his father, James, since the beginning of his life. Years later, Dalvin would talk about how much he loved his dad and how close they were. He would follow his dad around on his various tasks and through his various meetings and started to soak up his personality and larger-than-life, friendly, joyful smile, laugh, and attitude.

"Everywhere my daddy went, I wanted to go," Dalvin said. "I was always up under him, and it was like that when I got older, too. I just always wanted to stay with my dad."

To know James Cook was to love him. He really was the sort of person who took the air out of a room, attracted attention, and made new friends in no time. James had a mobile car wash and was a big fan of playing loud Jamaican music. He was known for his love: Chinese chicken fried rice was a favorite meal, but he could make almost anything in the kitchen. He loved to eat, he loved to cook, he loved to make others laugh and tell stories, and meet new people and learn their stories.

James made quite the impression on his kids, and his attitude and outlook on life did as well. Because of that, his children appreciated the simple joys of life. They also believed that they should do whatever they love. It doesn't matter if they wanted to be musicians, doctors, astronauts, run a car wash or be the president. No matter what you do, James told his kids, do it well. Do it with passion. Do it with joy. Don't listen to what other people say.

Your only limitations, James told his children, are in your mind. The only roadblocks that can stop you are the ones you set yourself.

Dalvin and his brothers and sisters learned something else from their father: your actions and words speak for themselves. The way you carry and show yourself to others is a true and honest representation of you. You need to consider how you appear to others, as well as how your actions come across to others.

This idea would definitely come back into Dalvin's life again and again.

Dalvin's young life was one full of great activities, such as being outdoors and experiencing a somewhat wild and extravagant life, even as a child. He would spend time with his mom and siblings, cooking meals together, playing games, and roughhousing in the backyard. And he would also travel around Florida with his dad, learning pieces of homegrown wisdom and becoming a smaller version of his dad.

It was a good life, but it was one that got a bit complicated at times.

A Major Move

Dalvin's home life wasn't always easy. Like many big families with limited income, Dalvin's parents were forced to make choices that were best for their children but not always the most comfortable and happy at the time. This led to him being apart from some of his family members, but it also allowed him to get much closer to someone who would change his life forever.

At the age of 13, the future running back moved in with his grandmother, who was lovingly known in the town as Miss Betty. She was the Little League team parent, and she spent her own money to bake dozens of peanut butter and jelly sandwiches to give to Cook's teammates after games.

It was around this time that Dalvin became convinced that he had a serious future in the world of professional sports. Already, he had played games throughout his youth and it was obvious that physically he was going to be very imposing and powerful.

But he was a piece of coal that would need to be pressured into becoming a diamond.

Living with Miss Betty, as well as the inspiration and drive he received from his family throughout his life, made Dalvin to focus on playing football in high school.

But he knew that if he was going to follow this path, he was going to commit himself 100% to it. His dad had taught him to fully invest in his talents and his joys and goals. Therefore, if he was going to play football, he was going to be the best football player he could be.

Yes, he had the physical build that could make him a good player, but did he have the skill and the knowledge, and the understanding of the game? Not yet. Luckily for Dalvin, he was a fast, dedicated learner and his father was someone who had always loved the game.

With the help of his dad, his family, and himself, Dalvin started down a path to become a future NFL superstar. It all started when he was about to enter high school, as Dalvin turned to the NFL and studied the game and the players dominating it.

Dalvin was a young man when he became very interested in playing football. In some ways, it was a chance for him to set himself apart from a big, boisterous family. He could be a star, gain more attention, and make a name for himself.

In other ways, it was just something he felt drawn to. He was a strong kid. At the time, he was quiet and kind but was quickly becoming a gentle giant. If he wanted to, he could become a special type of football player who had immense power and strength.

He had liked football all his life and was particularly drawn to the position of the running back. It seemed like the perfect way for him to combine his drive to do great and his strength and power. It would all come together.

Choosing the right path for himself in football was tricky because he really could have taken multiple career paths in football. Anyone who is fast and strong has a foot in the door. So knowing that, Dalvin just had to narrow down his choices and figure out what sort of player he wanted to be. Did he want to be the type of player who would crash into others, cause havoc and do damage to the defense? Did he want to be someone who was smart and fast and all about helping other players score?

Or did he want to do both?

All of this led him to the position of the running back. Once he started studying the game and began to understand what a running back does, something inside him clicked and it became obvious that this was the right choice for him.

What is it about this role that called out to Dalvin? And how did the young player start to change his style—and his body—in order to become the very best running back around?

Dreaming Of Being A Running Back

It's undeniable that one of the most visible key spots on a football team is running back. It is also one of the most difficult ones to become great at as well. While many children want to be great running backs in the National Football League, only a small percentage reach that level, with fewer people staying there for a long time. It's a position in the game that can chew even the best players up and spit them out. In other words, it's not for the faint of heart or the weak-willed. It's a position that requires dedication, know-how, strength, and a desire to always grow, get better, and never rest.

Playing Running Back in the NFL is not for the faint of heart, the NFL's average career is just over three years but the average playing duration for men who are running backs in the league is hardly over two and a half years. Although it doesn't look like a big deal at first glance, that's a significant decline in lifetime average compared to the league average.

So, why don't running backs in the NFL last that long?

There are a number of elements at play, but the truth that running backs suffer a hammering on almost every play is one of the most common.

Between both the times he carries the ball and receives the ball as a receiver, a prominent running back on a team might carry the ball somewhere between 15 to 30 times every game. And he'll take a hit from a defender on almost each one of those possessions.

So, if the running back goes out of bounds or scores a touchdown, a defender is almost certain to have interacted with him in a rough way.

Therefore, even if the running back somehow gets away unharmed, he's undoubtedly made a lot of quick cuts that will create wear and tear on his knees, hips, back, and more. Dalvin knew all of this as he became engrossed with football and, surprisingly, it didn't scare him away. Part of that had to do with the fact that he was a big guy for being a teenager. But he was also being supported by his father, Miss Betty, and his brothers and sisters. They told him that, yes, he could get roughed up on the field, but he could also be the best one out there.

Dalvin would later admit that he wasn't even sure of the responsibilities of a running back when he started to pursue it. There was a lot of ambiguity in his mind about what he'd be tasked with and what he'd have to do if he followed this path. But he soon learned a lot about the position and the way he would have to play the game. A running back is responsible for scooping up charging defending players and stopping them on their driven, furious pass plays. A running back is also the target of each defensive player in the game and is laser-focused on stopping him when he grabs the football.

As you can see, being a running back isn't simple, but it's still a fantastic position to start and can be highly gratifying. Plus, it can be the difference-maker for many teams in the NFL. Yes, being a running back is a challenging job and one that can absolutely wipe you out both physically and mentally, but it's also a great way to be put in the limelight.

Dalvin wanted that. Yes, he was young and, no, he didn't have any experience playing professional ball and limited experience playing anything even less than that. But even at a young age, he knew he was capable of carrying a heavy load. He knew he was ready to be a team player. And honestly, he knew he could handle the fame, pressure, and the fanbase rooting him on...or jeering him when he failed.

Maybe it was the way he was raised. Maybe it was his desire to break from the pack of his siblings. Maybe it was just something that he picked up from watching professional sports and seeing how athletes can be heroes to so many. Whatever the reason, Dalvin was sure that he could be an incredible running back.

But before he could do that, he had to hit the books and study the game and the position that would someday make him a star.

One of the first things Dalvin learned was how steep the learning curve would be and how much he was going to have to perfect his game and his body in order to achieve his goals. Most excellent running backs possess a set of characteristics and abilities that distinguish them from other players in their position. Running backs, like quarterbacks, must continuously monitor the field for openings and take on duties.

Running backs, unlike quarterbacks, must do all of this while running through crowds. To notice openings in the defense, a running back has to have excellent vision. A running back also needs to be able to monitor the field with his peripheral vision in order to spot these gaps.

What Dalvin learned right out of the gate was that the running back position is one of the most consequential—but rewarding—ones on the field. It was a complete rebuttal to people who claim that football players aren't smart or don't have a lot of foresight. Those who think that football is a dumb man's game clearly haven't studied what running backs do.

Even Dalvin would later admit that he wasn't sure of the roles and responsibilities that could come his way until he dug deep into what the position of running back had to offer and ask of him.

Something that really did appeal to him at that age was that the game was going to demand that he become intelligent and driven, and also capable of possessing foresight and deep and critical thinking abilities. He was going to need high intelligence to be aware of where he was going even if he couldn't see it.

This appealed to Dalvin because it was once again a chance to impress his family and show that he had something special inside of him. He was more than a strong, powerful presence; he had a brain too. He was the type of kid that was always proud of his grades and always felt good when his mother or father, or grandmother commended him for doing well in school. It felt good to be intelligent and the thought of being able to carry that into the world of sports was very exciting and appealing to him.

A Work Ethic To Match The Dream

Intelligence is one of those characteristics that can't just be learned or coached even by the most professional staff. Indeed, it is a trait that someone develops over time after having the position and seeing the game up close and personal for years. Dalvin, luckily, was always considered a smart kid. Part of this was just natural; he had good genes. But another part of it was the call and demands of his father, James. His dad would consistently say that Dalvin should never settle for less and should never stop learning. It didn't have to be about science or math, but James encouraged—almost demanded—that his children remain curious, like students of the world.

That's the way James was. He learned a lot of things, contained multitudes of knowledge, and was always looking to gain some new information about any number of topics. He wanted the same for his kids, including Dalvin.

So as the young boy studied the game of football, he looked at it as an assignment. He approached it like he would approach school and really became a student of the game. It was going to make him a better player and, eventually, it was going to make him a famous football player.

Yet, using knowledge and intelligence to study teams, plays, and recognize the gaps in defense isn't enough.

There is an undeniable physical aspect of playing football, especially playing the part of the running back. And Dalvin had to be aware of that, and be comfortable with it too.

This is because once someone in Dalvin's position has spotted the running hole, he must blast through it while evading tacklers. As you can imagine, this won't be an easy task. Dalvin was still a teenager when he first immersed himself in football. In other words, he was still growing. But it was very obvious that he could be a strong, commanding physical player. He was just about five foot ten inches when he was approaching high school and was weighing close to two hundred pounds. Yes, he was going to be someone who could throw his weight around on the field.

That was going to be important; the position of running back isn't just about reading the field and the opposition and finding holes in the defense. It's also about running like hell through those holes, even when multiple massive men are trying to block your path, slow you down, and tear you apart.

Dalvin would need to be fearless. He would need to be ready—eager, even—to throw himself headfirst into the fray and let himself get roughed up. Thank goodness for helmets, he thought. He would be nothing without his brain and he was going to be putting it at risk again and again every time he saw an opportunity and ran right for it on the football field.

Because of the immense physical demands of the position, a running back should have strong leg muscles and core, be swift, and be able to adapt to change rapidly in order to do this. A running back should make a bunch of rapid side-to-side motions before sprinting straight ahead as fast as he can. Even the strongest running backs must be able to evade being tackled or struck.

All of this meant that Dalvin was going to need to push his mind to the limit but also push his body to the limit. He wasn't old, but it was time for him to hit the gym and gain more strength since he wanted to play as a running back, which requires both a sharp mind and a strong body. He could settle for nothing less than excellence. And that would require a lot of work, a lot of long nights, and exhausting days.

He would go to school, he would run laps, he would work out, and he would study football. He would eat, he would sleep, he would wake up, shower, and do it all over again. A schedule like that is intense on a fully-grown man. But for a young teen? It can absolutely wipe them out.

Not Dalvin. He fondly remembers days when he would wake early, have breakfast with his grandmother and then head outside to start a day of mental and physical training. He was ready for it. He knew it was worth it. He knew it was providing him the sort of body and mind he would need to become a superstar on the field.

A running back's main responsibility after he catches the ball is to avoid tackles. Great running backs will use a variety of movements to make opponents miss, such as the stutter step, hurdle, stiff arm, spin move, or juke. All of these actions need a blend of quickness, speed, power, and agility.

Again, this was an instance of Dalvin using his brain to commend and compliment and carry his body. He knew that he would need to be physically fit and imposing to get the job done. But what about the strategy and the knowledge of knowing when to move toward an opponent or run away? When to spin, when to jump, when to dodge? All of that was really a task of the mind. Those were the things that his brain and knowledge of the game would help him work on. His body would just follow what his mind commanded. So, it made even more sense for Dalvin to continue looking at the game as an assignment— a challenge waiting to be met and conquered.

The majority of the outstanding running backs will establish their techniques after many games and much experience, as they determine how to stay upright the most. As for Dalvin, he was figuring it out quickly—very quickly. His family and friends commented that he was taking to the game faster than anyone else they had ever seen. It was almost as if he was naturally born to play. It was almost as if he had found his purpose.

That's how Dalvin felt, and the more he trained and the closer high school got, the more assured he was that he was making the right choice and was on a path that was going to take him not just to college but also to the NFL.

A running back needs to be capable of taking a lot of knocks while pulling himself up again and again, no matter how bruised, battered, and tired he is. Every time he runs, his aim is to score a touchdown. Of course, touchdown on every play is unlikely, but he should strive to get as many yards as possible on each carry. With that in mind, Dalvin spent countless hours in the hot Florida sun practicing drills, pushing his body to the breaking point, and building up his mass, muscles, and stamina. He was ready to face opponents head-on. He was becoming a beast, especially for his age, and was looking like someone quite a few years older than him.

One of the things he prided himself on in those early days was his ability to evade other defensive players as much as possible, in addition to searching for gaps and cutting to different sections of the football field, and battling for extra yards after the initial contact. He knew that he would have more ways to make a big impact on his team.

He had studied the game like a student studied school lessons or, more accurately, like a chess fan studies the masters of the board. With all of that in mind, as well as the support of his family, friends, and most especially his father, Dalvin radically changed his body and improved his knowledge of the game and how to conquer it. He felt like he was ready to move to high school and become a player that could gain the interest of colleges and, a few years after that, the NFL too.

But he also knew that competition to get on the team would be tough.

He was in Florida and in the part of the state he resided in, high school football was king. Millions of people were obsessed with the game and, therefore, not just anyone could make their way onto the high school field. Schools took the selection of players very seriously. It was a cutthroat and demanding process, and Dalvin knew that he would be one of many vying for a spot on the team.

Notwithstanding, he had faith. As he entered high school, the young player was more physically built and mentally acute than most other kids his age. He knew that gave him a huge leg up. But his transformation into a high school football hero wouldn't come without a few bumps in the road.

STARTING HIGH SCHOOL

Dalvin, like many other kids in the area, entered high school with some trepidation and fear. But his anxieties weren't just about fitting in and making friends and not being an outcast. They were also about being a football player.

Dalvin went to Miami Central High School, a very popular school that was also home to future legendary Seminole running back, Devonta Freeman. That just goes to show the sort of impressive roster of talent that was learning and playing alongside him. It also shows how competitive it would be to make the team.

Dalvin had high hopes for his future when he entered high school, but his hopes were quickly dashed and he found himself doubting his talent and abilities, not for the first or last time in his life.

In fact, he felt that his own chances were so low that he didn't even attempt to make the football team. He felt that the roster was already too crowded with too many talents, and he didn't even want to make any attempt and risk feeling like a failure or ridiculed. It's wild to think about it now because he is such a huge presence in the NFL and easily one of the best running backs alive, but Cook didn't join the football team until his sophomore year, thinking that he wouldn't be able to replace the team's running back, Devonta Freeman, who was behind

Miami Central making it to the Class 6A state championship in 2010.

Dalvin saw that the team already had a stunning, one-of-a-kind running back, so he felt that his chances of making the cut were slim. Or he imagined that he would sit on the sidelines all season, which, to him, was a fate worse than not making it all. So, he just sat out his freshman year and started to focus on playing in his second year.

But he didn't just sit on his hands and not do anything during that first year of high school. Quite the opposite, in fact. He spent that time perfecting his game even more. He actually based a lot of what he was doing off of Devonta Freeman after watching him play and seeing him lead the team to victory repeatedly.

GETTING STRONGER

Dalvin knew that he was smart as he entered high school, but he wasn't completely confident or satisfied with his physical strength or abilities, especially after seeing Freeman play for the high school team. Therefore, he went back to the gym to get himself in even better shape.

You may be under the assumption that working on speed is the most important task a running back needs to tackle, yet speed is a difficult skill to teach and master. You are either born with it or you don't. Or, you've learned how to master it at a young age. Yes, speed is a vital part of being a running back. Thankfully, Dalvin already had that skill and was quick, athletic, and ready to move.

However, he did need to work on getting stronger. Being an excellent running back means you need to have superior strength, and Dalvin wasn't satisfied with his power.

He knew how he could do this. Dalvin could invest in working out and gaining muscle in his upper, lower, and core body to make himself better suited for the football team and capable of actually making an impression on his coach.

Getting stronger at such a young age was going to help him stop tacklers and aid his development of durability, helping him to withstand a lot of contact on the field.

But if he wanted to surpass Freeman and every other player in the area, he also needed to be extremely active every time he was out on the field because it was obvious that playing in the hot Florida sun was going to continually tire him out. Dalvin was well aware that he needed to work on his endurance in order to be ready for his high school goals. This was going to be accomplished through a lot of sprinting, jogging, as well as brisk walking.

This immediately increased his body's capacity for activity and prevented him from being too exhausted during the game.

He also had his eyes on getting better at his flexibility and dexterity. Staying low to the ground is important for running backs so they can rush right through gaps in the defense, plus discover opportunities on the football field, and pick up defenders on blocks.

The lower these players can go, the higher the probability of being effective and victorious. Dalvin's goal was to master the appropriate posture in an attempt to stay as low to the ground as possible.

To impress his coach even more, Dalvin also studied his fellow players and got better at achieving handoffs. One of the most basic skills a running back has to possess is the ability to take a handoff. However, it is not a natural talent, particularly when performed at a rapid pace throughout a game.

Taking a successful handoff requires a certain technique, which requires considerable experience. And that is exactly what Dalvin wanted to show his coach: experience, ability, knowledge, and the sort of adaptability that would make him a great starting running back.

A High School Hero

Sure enough, when his sophomore year rolled around, Dalvin was impressing those in power and was proving that all his hard work, studying, and dedication to the game had paid off.

Coach Telly Lockette used Cook as a running back as well as a defensive back. Right away, he was a pivotal part of the team and became a vital feature that Coach Lockette used again and again. Not only was Dalvin in the good books of the coaching staff, but he also made friends. Everyone knows that getting close with other students is a major part of high school and makes the whole experience much easier. Luckily for Dalvin, he was becoming close with many of the guys he was playing with. In fact, he participated in carries with his best friend, Joseph Yearby, in his junior year.

Yearby lined up as the quarterback on running downs, while Cook lined up as a running back. They made an excellent pairing together and it was Dalvin's first experience of really messing with a teammate, something that would come in handy in a huge way when he made it to college and then the NFL.

When his high school came to an end, Dalvin had a whole lot to be proud of. He got a late start on the game because he sat out his freshman year, but he made a considerable impact on the team and his own future too.

In the end, Dalvin ran for 1,940 yards and 34 touchdowns through a total of 177 runs as a senior in 2013, and he also intercepted three passes on defense. Cook rushed for 244 yards and three touchdowns in Miami Central's Class 6A regional championship victory over Palm Bay Heritage despite Yearby's fibula fracture in the first quarter.

But that wasn't all. Dalvin's record was far more impressive than that. He also helped his team get to the Class 6A state title, in which he ran a total of 220 yards as well as four touchdowns in a 52–7 triumph over Seffner Armwood, giving his squad their latest state championship in four years and making them the first Dade team to reach four straight state finals.

Because of all this, Dalvin was voted Mr. Florida Football by the Florida Dairy Farmers Association for his season efforts, becoming the third Miami-Dade County resident to receive the accolade since its foundation, following previous Miami Northwestern quarterback, Jacory Harris, and past Miami Norland running back icon, Duke Johnson.

All in all, Cook led Miami Central to a 52–5 record throughout his high school career, running for 4,267 yards and 64 touchdowns. His senior season honors included being named to the All-USA Football Team from the publication, USA Today, as well as 247Sports Second Team All-American, and first-team All-State Class 6A. Following that, Cook was asked to play in the 2014 Under Armor All-America Game after his senior season, where he carried for 78 yards, plus a touchdown on only eight rushes for

Team Nitro. Cook was also a part of "The Opening," a Nike Campus all-star summer prospect camp.

These were all huge indicators that Cook was making major waves in the world of high school football. His time in high school was far better than just about anyone in the local area, or the state as a whole. This meant that his prospects of getting drafted by a good college were immense and he was well on his way to being a collegiate athlete.

The accolades kept on coming for Dalvin as he got ready to graduate. Rivals.com, for example, rated Dalvin as the second strongest all-purpose back in his class, giving him a five-star rating. He was eager to move out of high school and straight into college. Once again, his knowledge and intelligence were helping him in that aspect. He had already completed the summer and night studies required to finish high school prematurely and participate in the spring semester when he registered with Florida State in January 2014.

His choice of going with Florida State at first seemed like a match made in heaven and something that would be hugely beneficial to both Dalvin and the college. But it looked like FSU wasn't his first pick. He was actually pledged to Clemson University first, but in the spring of 2013, he switched to the University of Florida due to his desire to play under coach Will Muschamp. Following Florida's 4–8 season that year, though, the 5-star running back began to doubt his commitment in private. However, those private doubts about the school somehow became public and it created the first—and most minor—controversy of Dalvin's career.

But the controversy was short-lived and Cook eventually came back to his choice and stopped doubting his future with FSU. Despite formally visiting other colleges, Cook eventually stated that he was "100 percent" devoted to the University of Florida. To really show his commitment, he did the "Gator Chomp" on social media and posed for photographs with Florida recruits after one of the workout sessions.

And that was that. Dalvin transferred to Florida State University on January 1, 2014, and started his illustrious and powerful time with the school. It would end up being a huge step on his way to the NFL.

A Rough Start To Life As A Seminole

From 2014 through 2016, Dalvin was a member of Florida State's football team, where he played super well for head coach, Jimbo Fisher.

As a freshman in 2014, Cook carried for 67 yards and a score in his debut game against The Citadel. Against the very difficult opponent, Syracuse, Dalvin also carried for 100 yards for the very first time in his college years, accumulating 122 yards on 23 touches and one running score.

Right off the bat, Dalvin became well known among college football fans, analysts, and experts. Dalvin was voted the ACC Championship Game MVP after gaining a career-high 177 yards on 31 attempts and one running score against Georgia Tech. In total, he had 1,008 running yards, along with eight rushing touchdowns, 22 catches, and 203 receiving yards in the 2014 season. Those are incredible numbers and they showed that the very same player who was doing such great work in high school had turned into a powerful, promising, and uncompromising college player too.

However, a huge speed bump was coming, and it was because of Dalvin himself. It was also something that could completely derail or end his college career.

Unfortunately, Dalvin was a part of three different off-field incidents with the law during his first year at FSU.

Dalvin made some major mistakes in his first few years at Florida State. As a teenager who was away from home for the first time he made multiple poor choices that would lead to many in the press condemning him and calling for his expulsion.

Dalvin made some major mistakes and was forced to face the ramifications of these choices. Dalvin did not make any statements about his legal situation on advice of his lawyers, but it's clear to see that he was very sorry for his poor choices.

The fact was that his future at the school and in the NFL was certainly in question after these legal issues. What NFL teams would be willing to take on a player with such heavy baggage? Even if he was a great college player, was his talent enough for teams within the league to turn a blind eye? That was a lot to ask for a league that already had a bad rap for allowing violent people to play in it.

To this day, Dalvin is still very quiet about the problems he had with the law. It is obvious that he was hoping to turn a page, put the past behind him, and focus on football. After his first law enforcement problems at FSU, he was desperate to get back to the field and do what he did best: play ball.

And, after a long break, that's what he did.

Return To The Field

Dalvin had 156 running yards and a rushing score against Texas State to start the season. He had missed a lot of time because of his legal issues, but he was back and he was obviously back with a vengeance. He was ready to play and earn his keep and show people that he was far more than just nasty headlines in the newspaper.

Dalvin gained 266 running yards, plus three rushing touchdowns in the next game against South Florida. 266 running yards is an awful lot, even for a very accomplished running back. But that was Dalvin just warming up, just getting started, just shaking the rust off, and getting back to his normal pace. Shortly after his 266-yard game, he gained 222 running yards and two rushing touchdowns against the Miami Hurricanes on October 10, coupled with 47 receiving yards and a catching touchdown to help the Seminoles reach a 5–0 record.

Cook was playing better than ever before and was starting to win records that were set by some of the best college players to ever suit up and take to the football field. In fact, Dalvin beat Warrick Dunn's Florida State single-season running yards record of 1,242 yards during the team's eleventh game, which was against NC State. He rushed for 183 yards and two scores in the annual nationally televised game versus the Florida Gators.

Altogether, he has 1,691 running yards, 19 rushing touchdowns, 24 catches, 244 receiving yards, and one receiving score in the 2015 season. The season began with some serious legal issues and how they would affect his time at FSU and his future in the NFL, but he had quickly put those fears to rest with the way he was playing. Yes, he had made some huge mistakes and, yes, FSU was questioning whether they wanted to expel him or not. But there was no question that Dalvin was back and performing like the athlete everyone knew he was.

As the 2016 season rolled around, Dalvin was ready to build on the success he found in 2015. That's exactly what he did, right out the gate. In a win over Ole Miss, Cook had 91 running yards with 101 receiving yards to start the 2016 season.

Following that, Dalvin surpassed his incredible 266-yard game with 267 running yards, in addition to two rushing touchdowns and 62 receiving yards against South Florida on September 24. He recorded 140 running yards with three rushing touchdowns in the following game against North Carolina, as well as six receptions, totaling 106 yards.

Once again, Dalvin was surging with his team and, once again, he was breaking records. Ironically, he broke another record set by FSU great, Warrick Dunn. Dalvin broke Dunn's career running record of 3,959 yards on November 19, 2016, in the first part of the team's game against the Syracuse Orange.

It was time for Dalvin to make a choice. He had only spent three years at FSU and could decide to stick it out for his senior year. He was sure to break more records, make more fans, and perfect his game even more.

However, he was well aware that the NFL was calling. And he was also well aware that he could take the leap and enter the league before his official time at Florida State was over. What was driving his choice to possibly abandon his school and start his professional career? It was mostly the fact that football is a young man's game. Already, Dalvin had experienced the wear and tear that comes with playing ball at that level. It all adds up and can have a devastating impact on a player's body. Therefore, the longer he played in college, the more wear he'd suffer if he entered the NFL.

He knew there was a lot of interest from some big NFL teams and that was music to Dalvin's ear. He was excited to try his hand in the big league, especially considering the legal problems he had suffered just a few years ago. The fact that there were still teams that wanted him was huge and impressive and made him feel amazing, talented, and worthwhile.

So, the choice was actually easy to make: Dalvin wanted to leave FSU and start his time in the NFL.

When his time at Florida ended, Dalvin had a total of 4,464 running yards. Cook officially announced that he would forego his last year with Florida State so he could join the

2017 NFL Draft only hours after winning the Orange Bowl versus Michigan.

THE NFL COMBINE

Dalvin was a hot commodity in the league and was attracting a lot of attention even before the NFL draft. He was easily one of the best college players around and there were countless teams within the league that saw a way to capitalize on his power, skills, and intelligence.

Because of this, Cook was invited to the NFL combine and went through all the compulsory combine activities as well as positional drills. He did the 40- and 20-yard dashes, plus the 10-yard dash, and other substantial and performative exercises at Florida State's Pro Day.

He was impressing everyone who watched him. He was definitely one of the most exciting prospective draft picks. The NFL combine is a place where players can strut their stuff, show their skills, and showcase their potential for growth. The media was already going nuts for Dalvin. In fact, Sports Illustrated and Pro Football Focus regarded him as the best running back in that year's draft, while NFL media analysts placed him high above the list of potential players.

But there were concerns, and his past choices once again reared their ugly heads. Although he was regarded as one of the best running backs in the league, off-the-field difficulties, such as his past arrests, concerns about his personality and character, his fumbling problems, and a few instances of shoulder ailments lowered his stock. The NFL at that time was grappling with other players who had faced similar legal issues and they were looking to change their ways and not be a league that seemingly approved of, or turned a blind eye to, the violent actions of some of its players. To say there was some discomfort with the prospect of Dalvin joining the league was an understatement. There were, in fact, some people who were openly protesting the idea.

Despite all that hesitation and protests against him, Dalvin was expected to be picked in the opening rounds of the NFL draft, according to experts and pundits.

THE DRAFT

In the end, Dalvin was chosen 41st overall in the second round of the 2017 NFL Draft by the Minnesota Vikings. After Leonard Fournette and fellow player, Christian McCaffrey, Dalvin was the third running back selected in that year's draft.

It's hard to make your way into the NFL Draft. There are countless players across the country and across the world hoping to get picked who don't make it, for many reasons. The fact that Dalvin had been drafted was the realization of a life dream and something that he once didn't even consider possible. He had made no secret about the fact that he would sometimes doubt himself, even with all the success he had found in high school and college.

He also made no secret of the fact that he thought too much controversy surrounded him. There were times when he legitimately didn't think he'd get drafted because of the legal issues he had created for himself.

So, when he was called to the Minnesota Vikings, it felt like a true blessing and a chance for Dalvin to once again turn the page and devote himself even more to a sport he loved and a team that believed in him.

Right away, he was showing that the Vikings made the right choice by selecting him. Cook claimed the Vikings' rookie debut running record, formerly held by Adrian Peterson, by rushing for 127 yards on 22 runs in his inaugural NFL match-up versus the New Orleans Saints.

Sure enough, his first season with the Viking was a very important and impressive one for the young Florida native. Fans were impressed by Dalvin, and his jersey started to sell, as he consistently kept the team alive in some tough games.

He racked up 27 runs for 97 yards and a score in Week 3 when pitted against the Tampa Bay Buccaneers, as well as five receptions for 72 yards.

Injury Strikes

It was a great showing for the young star and it looked like he might be the breakout rookie star of the season. But then something drastic, damaging, and dangerous happened and it sidetracked Dalvin immediately. He was forced to leave the game against the Detroit Lions in Week 4 with a probable knee injury.

The growing Dalvin Cook fanbase collective held its breath to hear how bad the injury was and what it meant for his future with the team and the Vikings' chances for the year. Then the bad news struck: just one day after the injury, it was confirmed that Cook had torn his ACL, which ended his rookie season early.

It didn't end like he expected but Dalvin's rookie year was one for the history books and was incredibly promising. Dalvin ultimately rushed for 354 yards in four games during his rookie season. He was showing that he had easlly made the leap from college football to professional football with total grace. He was definitely a young player to look out for, someone who could eventually have a long and successful career in the NFL.

Cook's left ACL was successfully repaired on October 9, 2017. An orthopedic specialist said there was no more damage to the left knee and that it had a "100 percent" possibility of returning to its healed state for the 2018 season.

That meant one thing: Dalvin Cook was back, and he was once again ready to make up for lost time. If his previous forced absences from the field were any indication, he was about to play like a man with a mission.

Return To The Field

Cook recorded 95 scrimmage yards in the first contest of the season, his first game back following his season-ending injury, in a 24–16 victory over the San Francisco 49ers. It looked like he was back and better than ever. It felt like his injuries were behind him.

But that sadly wasn't the case.

Cook tore his hamstring in Week 2 and missed the Vikings' next four games after playing through it in Week 4 with 10 carries. This was sadly becoming a pattern for Dalvin. He was playing a tough position in a very tough game and it was costing his body again and again. However, few people expected him to be facing so many injuries after entering the league.

Thankfully, the latest injury didn't sideline him for the entire year and he was able to return to the field in no time. After an 89-yard return in Week 9, he had relatively minimal success in the following three games. He recorded 84 running yards and eight catches in a Week 13 defeat to the Patriots. Cook was obviously a bit impaired following his injury but he was still named NFC Offensive Player of the Week after running for 136 yards and his sole two rushing touchdowns in a 41–17 takedown of Miami's Dolphins in Week 15.

Cook concluded the 2018 season with 615 running yards and two touchdowns, which surpassed backup, Latavius

Murray, even though he had less touches. He also had 305 yards plus two scores on 40 catches.

THE 2019 SEASON

As the 2019 year began, Dalvin was looking to have a season free of injury or sitting on the bench. He had already gained legions of fans and had won multiple awards because of his hard work and he was sick and tired of sitting by and letting his team down because of injuries.

He wanted a full season of true power and showing off his potential. He felt like he owed it to his team, his fans, and himself.

He got off to a terrific start, yet again. Cook carried 21 times for 111 yards as well as two touchdowns in the Vikings' 28–12 win over the Atlanta Falcons in the season opener. Following that tremendous start, he kept it going. Dalvin carried for 154 yards and a 75-yard touchdown run against the Green Bay Packers in Week 2 of the Vikings' 16–21 loss.

2019 was shaping up to be something really special right away. Dalvin seized the league lead in running yards, the first time he had achieved such a feat. Cook impressed the fans and the league when he ran 16 times for 110 yards and one score in the Vikings' 34–14 win over the Oakland Raiders in Week 3. He also grabbed four catches for 33 yards.

Week after week, Dalvin was impressing those watching the game. He had 132 running yards and 86 receiving yards in Week 5 against the New York Giants, giving him a total of 218 yards as the Vikings won 28–10. Cook rushed for 142 yards and two touchdowns in the Vikings' 42–30 win against the Detroit Lions in Week 7, retaking the league lead in running.

After that, Dalvin carried 23 times for 98 yards and a score in the next game—a 19 - 9 win against the then-Washington Redskins—and caught five catches for 73 yards. For his efforts and terrific start to the season, Dalvin was named NFC Offensive Player of the Week.

2020: A Difficult Season

It all seemed like things were going great for Dalvin and, because of him, the Minnesota Vikings. But, as so often happens in the NFL, a labor dispute was brewing between the two sides.

Dalvin felt that he has proven himself repeatedly to the Viking's front office, the fans, and the league. Because of that, he felt that he deserved more money for his work. Dalvin was ready to get paid more and he took to the press to state his case and put the Vikings in a very difficult spot.

 Cook said on June 8, 2020 that he will refrain from participating in team-related activities until a "reasonable extension" is reached. This sort of standstill didn't happen often and it created tons of headlines and bad press, both for the Vikings and for Dalvin himself. Some people said the Vikings should easily upgrade the contract and pay Dalvin more. Meanwhile, other people were saying that Dalvin was being a sore sport and a bad team player and was letting the rest of his squad down by not suiting up.

Thankfully, the whole situation didn't last too long and it worked out for both sides. Cook then agreed to a multi-year, $63 million dollar package deal with the Vikings on September 12, 2020.

As the new season started, it looked like it was going to be his best yet. He had restructured his contract and was happy and comfortable with his future with the team. It looked like things were in better standing than ever before and he was ready to once again impress the fans and make them proud.

He also wanted to make his dad proud. His entire football career had revolved around his dad, who had encouraged him to try hard and believe in himself even from the very beginning.

Unfortunately, his father wouldn't live to see the end of this latest season.

On December 29, 2020, Dalvin received a call from his grandmother, Betty, saying that she had found Dalvin's father lifeless on his bed. Despite the use of CPR, Dalvin's dad, James, didn't respond even as paramedics were on the way.

However, it was too late. The EMTs arrived and did all they could but James was lost, dead at just 46 from complications due to diabetes.

The news hit Dalvin like a ton of bricks. He pulled over to the side of the road and sobbed, remembering how important his dad was to him. He recalled the times he spent practicing in the sun with his father and the laughs and joy they shared. He remembered all the wisdom his father gave him, the great advice, and the encouragement. Through good times and bad, Dalvin's dad was always there for him. Now, sadly, he was gone.

Dalvin wanted to make his father proud, even though he had passed away. He was already having a terrific season with the Vikings but he knew that it was going to be even more important and close to his heart now. He could still feel his father, his support, wisdom, and guidance. In a way, he now knew that his dad would be sitting by the sidelines for every game moving forward.

A Bright Future

Dalvin Cook has been through a lot. He has suffered injuries and setbacks, both because of bad luck and because of his own actions. He has also experienced great success because of his belief in himself and his hard work and determination to be the very best.

Dalvin is a prime example of the shortcomings and potential of professional athletes. They are not perfect people. They have problems and issues, and they make major mistakes, like we all do. But they also get far in life because of their dedication and belief. They do not quit.

Dalvin Cook hasn't quit. Through thick and thin, ups and downs, and good times and bad, he has pressed himself, pushed himself, and always fought to be better and reach higher heights in his career.

That's why he's such a pivotal part of the Minnesota Vikings and the NFL.

MORE FROM JACKSON CARTER BIOGRAPHIES

My goal is to spark the love of reading in young adults around the world. Too often children grow up thinking they hate reading because they are forced to read material they don't care about. To counter this we offer accessible, easy to read biographies about sportspeople that will give young adults the chance to fall in love with reading.

Go to the Website Below to Join Our Community

https://mailchi.mp/7cced1339ff6/jcbcommunity

Or Find Us on Facebook at

www.facebook.com/JacksonCarterBiographies

As a Member of Our Community You Will Receive:

First Notice of Newly Published Titles

Exclusive Discounts and Offers

Influence on the Next Book Topics

Don't miss out, join today and help spread the love of reading around the world!

OTHER WORKS BY JACKSON CARTER BIOGRAPHIES

Patrick Mahomes: The Amazing Story of How Patrick Mahomes Became the MVP of the NFL

Donovan Mitchell: How Donovan Mitchell Became a Star for the Salt Lake City Jazz

Luka Doncic: The Complete Story of How Luka Doncic Became the NBA's Newest Star

The Eagle: Khabib Nurmagomedov: How Khabib Became the Top MMA Fighter and Dominated the UFC

Lamar Jackson: The Inspirational Story of How One Quarterback Redefined the Position and Became the Most Explosive Player in the NFL

Jimmy Garoppolo: The Amazing Story of How One Quarterback Climbed the Ranks to Be One of the Top Quarterbacks in the NFL

Zion Williamson: The Inspirational Story of How Zion Williamson Became the NBA's First Draft Pick

Kyler Murray: The Inspirational Story of How Kyler Murray Became the NFL's First Draft Pick

Do Your Job: The Leadership Principles that Bill Belichick and the New England Patriots Have Used to Become the Best Dynasty in the NFL

Turn Your Gaming Into a Career Through Twitch and Other Streaming Sites: How to Start, Develop and Sustain an Online Streaming Business that Makes Money

From Beginner to Pro: How to Become a Notary Public

www.ingramcontent.com/pod-product-compliance
Lightning Source LLC
Chambersburg PA
CBHW060915130726
48001CB00006B/2250